GREAT WESTERN
BRANCH LINE ALBUM

GREAT WESTERN BRANCH LINE ALBUM

Ian Krause

LONDON
IAN ALLAN LTD

First published in 1969

Fifth impression 1974

ISBN 07110 0069 7

© *Ian Allan Ltd 1969*

Published by Ian Allan Ltd, Shepperton, Surrey and printed
in the United Kingdom by the Press at Coombelands Ltd.

PREFACE

"Up exe" said the station nameboard, with a kind of lyrical brevity. It was all I had imagined it to be, and it has become one of those nostalgic impulses one feels when one has nothing else to think about. Your mind wanders back to the flower beds in full bloom, the river Exe with its subtle shades of blue, the old train with the guard ringing the bell. It is the sort of memory that it is impossible to resist, because it spelt a peace which cannot now be simulated. How many hours were spent on holiday in the south west, soaking up a system of railways which belonged decades ago, a system which never changed except in the minor respect of engines.

The Great Western branch line was a thing apart, because, for the great part, it would run to serve a leisure public, or country workers. The ones that did not somehow lacked the charm of the more rural byway— the Exe Valley was not only beautiful because of its exterior beauty, but because of its travellers; the slow drawl of Devonian fat-stock prices on the 7.29 a.m. to Exeter, or the farmers' wives on the 4.30 p.m. return, knowing each other so well that you somehow felt that you were intruding in someone else's house. The "holiday lines" in Cornwall—St. Ives, Helston, Falmouth, Newquay; did not these strike a chord where say Staines (West) or Uxbridge did not? British sentimentality seems not least founded on sunshine and sea.

But there is always another side to the story—among the sun-drenched Up Exe's, there is always that filthy week of weather in 19 so and so at Portmadoc, or Kingswear, or Cardigan. And there are the forgotten lines— the lines which were built to make money all the year round; the lines most people try and forget. Coal trundling south from Aberdare to Cardiff, or from anywhere in South Wales to anywhere else. The valleys remained to

the end under-photographed. Their beauty could be astounding, but their reputation remained less so; compared with their Devonian and Mid-Welsh counterparts, their natural beauty provided more than a hundred Exe Valley's or Dart Valley's. But coal is a dirty word, and the Welsh image never had the lustre of elsewhere. A great deal too much was missed.

And so we went north, north through Torpantau with its low, slate grey skies and high rainfall, north to Central Wales, where the sunny memories can return. Three Cocks, Talyllyn, Tylwch, resonant to the sound of a Dean Goods; hills and footpaths rarely disturbed by the hordes heading west through Moat Lane towards Barmouth or Butlin's. Utterly still, basking in their lifeless beauty, these lines could not, and did not last. But the line to Butlin's has survived. The Cambrian coast line never seemed to be a branch line, in the most romantic sense of the word. There was always too much urgency as the double-headers blasted their exhaust skywards over Talerddig; there was something too down to earth in seeing lengthy trains snaking through Penrhyn-deudraeth towards Portmadoc and Pwllheli.

The photographers who approached these lines were many, but few came to terms with their subject. Beauty is not just an engine, it is the whole setting. What matter whether the engine is an 0-4-2 tank of years gone by or a standard post-1948 design? As long as it is steam, and as long as the viewer can associate the setting with his own memories, then the engine becomes immaterial. Following this preface, the man who, above all, came to terms with his subject, Ben Ashworth, has put into words some of his thoughts and ideas. He took trouble, and he got his results. A well-known railway photographer once said that he always put his camera away in winter. Look at the picture of an o–6–o climbing to Coleford in this book, and the futility of the statement becomes all too obvious.

For reasons of space, it has not been possible to include photographs of every branch line on the system; some lines have more coverage than others, because the photographs warrant it. I would like to thank everyone who has contributed to the book; I hope that it will in some way serve as a reminder of one of the pleasanter parts of the past years.

IAN KRAUSE

INTRODUCTION

MAKING A serious attempt at photographing branch line trains was an undertaking where all manner of incidents might crop up, some amusing, some hazardous and others just downright frustrating! However, before recalling a few of them, I thought it might be of interest to say why and how I set about taking my photographs.

To me the country branch line train passing to and fro within a stone's throw of my childhood home was a necessary part of life, in fact I could hardly have imagined being without it. Consequently, many years later, when it eventually became obvious that this way of life was to go, I naturally felt it would be a pity if it were to pass unrecorded as part of the country scene.

In recording it photographically I had to limit my equipment to a couple of second-hand 35 mm. Super Paxettes, with a light-weight touring bicycle as transport. Nevertheless I did have the good fortune to be living between the Cotswolds and Forest of Dean with some time off mid-week to explore those branch lines which, towards the end of their lives, ran Mon./Wed./Fri. only, (not forgetting 1420 on the Kington and Presteigne branches whose duties were otherwise arranged).

Like many other enthusiasts I wished I had taken up photography some ten years earlier, especially as time was fast running out for some of the branch lines by the time I got round to seeking out the characteristic scenes along each line. Undoubtedly the most interesting and tricky task was searching for the best viewpoint (frequently a tree top), and then lying in wait. Being a countryman at heart and something of an ornithologist, waiting, listening and watching in a remote spot, for perhaps the one train of the day, was rarely boring, although the time spent waiting often seemed out of all proportion to the mere couple of seconds when sun, wind and steam might or might not coincide to make the anticipated picture. Needless to say, frustration, disappointment and only a faint hope of better luck next time, were all to often my lot.

There is a saying "one picture is worth ten thousand words", nevertheless there are sights and sounds which cannot be recorded with a still camera, and it is often the more commonplace of these which come to mind when I think back . . .

. . . peering through frost patterned windows on January mornings, trying to weigh up the weather prospects before venturing out on the cold cycle ride to catch the first train to the Forest . . . or returning home of a Summer's afternoon on the 4 o'clock from Hereford, racing downhill between the orchards of Longhope, and above the rhythm of the wheels the characteristic sounds of a free wheeling Great Western loco wafting back through the open window.

Another unforgettable glimpse, typical of the same line . . . bursting from a cool narrow tunnel into blinding sunlight, and suddenly seeing, far below, the Wye with its carpets of water buttercups.

. . . a guard picking violets outside the tunnel entrance to Whitecliff Quarry, while the driver and fireman took refreshment (breakfast I think) on a sunny bank near their quietly simmering pannier tank.

. . . another guard, who after closing the gates behind his train was left stranded on a lonely crossing near Kington by an inattentive engine crew. Only after some hurried screwing down of the brake handle and much shouting by the other occupants of the van was the train (now lost to sight) halted and shunted back.

I have memories too of cycle-touring with

a stalwart companion in the Autumn rains and frosts of Mid-Wales . . . pitching our lightweight tent near the line at Erwood or Torpantau summit (but not so close as to be endangered by the hot cinders experienced near the latter!) . . . trying to steady a camera after a frantic last minute climb up slippery green branches and through shower laden leaves.

. . . or, the one that got away!—when I was caught unawares high above the entrance to Blue Rock Tunnel—a throbbing in the air—a subterranean rumbling, then suddenly, through the obscuring blast of hot blue fumes a brief glimpse of the outside cylinders and pounding con-rod of a G.W.R. 45xx tank, (the only time I ever saw that type of loco in the Forest of Dean). My camera was powerless to record, but I do still have the memory of that slow sharp exhaust beat echoing and re-echoing around the steep valley slopes.

. . . and on the Cotswolds . . . snakes basking on cuttings and embankments amongst the flowers and long flowing grasses . . . leaning over the sun warmed stonework of a country by-way bridge listening hopefully for the faint "ting-ting" from a distant signalbox—a shadowy movement within—a pause—the rattle of wires and the sound of a wooden signal arm dropping to clear.

So many of these once familiar sights and sounds are now gone, and I can only hope that for those who spare the time to turn them, these pages will bring similar pleasant memories—from the days before the present chaotic and dangerous motor-car age, which has brought about the downfall of a onetime solid, dependable and comparatively harmless way of life—The Great Western Branch Line.

B. J. ASHWORTH

2286 crosses the Wye at Kerne Bridge with a lightweight freight for Ross on Wye, on the evening of September 2, 1964.   [*E. J. S. Gadsden*

Crossing the River Glaslyn near Portmadoc—82033 and a 2251 0-6-0 on the
Pwllheli portion of the Cambrian Coast Express on September 9, 1961

[*M. J. Fox*

Above: 0–6–0T No. 2087 on a Princes Risborough to Watlington train leaving Aston Rowant in 1929   [*J. E. Kite*

Below: A pre-war shot on the Lambourn Valley line, with an 0–6–0 shedding its load

[*Len's of Sutton*

1447 basking in the beautiful summer of 1947 at Wallingford

[*H. C. Casserley*

Right: Devon in high summer—4570 on the 3.5pm Plymouth–Launceston somewhere near Plym Bridge on August 4, 1962 [S. C. Nash

Above: Outside frame 0–6–0PT No. 1570 waits at Tavistock with the Launceston–Plymouth train [Dr. Ian C. Allen

Below: 5569 coasts into Lydford in April 1961 on the same working [M. J. Esau

Right: The desolate wastes at Princetown alter little with the years. On June 15, 1926, 2–6–2T No. 4403 is running round its train in readiness for its return to Yelverton

[H. C. Casserley

Left: A South Molton–Taunton freight crossing the River Exe near Dulverton on August 28, 1961
                    [M. J. Fox

Right: TC Wolverhampton–Ilfracombe; 6363 leaving Dulverton on August 22, 1964
                    [M. J. Fox

Left: The 8.12am Barnstaple–Taunton wanders away from Wiveliscombe on the same day
                    [M. J. Fox

Right: 7333 climbs into the loop at Venn Cross with a Taunton-Barnstaple Junction freight, in August 1961
                    [M. J. Fox

B

Above: Water-stop at Halesowen in September 1966
[*John R. P. Hunt*

Left: Preserved 2251 No. 3205 crosses Oldbury Viaduct,
Bridgnorth, on the Severn Valley Line in April 1968
[*B. J. Ashworth*

19

Above: The last steam diagram on the branch. The 8.10am (SO) Taunton–Minehead takes the single line tablet at Bishop's Lydeard on August 22, 1964. The locos are 6148 and D6336   [*M. J. Fox*

Above: A Watchet–Taunton freight round the coast near Watchet in
September 1953 behind 0–6–0 No. 2275
[B. A. Butt

Below: 4157 climbs towards Washford with a Minehead to Taunton
train in August 1961   [M. J. Fox

Below: A spotless 2–6–2, No. 4593
leaves Washford on August 29,
1961 with a Taunton–Minehead
train   [M. J. Fox

Above: 0–4–2T No. 1465 waits to leave Yeovil Town for Pen Mill on May 21, 1935
[*H. C. Casserley*

Left: 6430 near Yeovil Town with an auto-train from Pen Mill in September 1964
[*M. J. Fox*

Below: 4591 coasts into Lyng Halt with the Yeovil–Taunton train in May 1964
[*M. J. Fox*

Left: Cheddar, looking east. 41203 is arriving with a train from Wells on May 13, 1960
[*E. T. Gill*

Below: The view from Clifton Suspension Bridge. The 5.30pm Bristol to Portishead is seen leaving Clifton Bridge station
[*S. Rickard*

Below, left: 41208 simmering at Wells (Tucker Street) after bringing a train from Yatton on June 16, 1962
[*M. J. Fox*

Above: 1631 being watered at Parkend in the Forest of Dean   [*B. J. Ashworth*

Left: 8701 leaving the tunnel at the entrance to Whitecliff Quarry on the former Coleford–Monmouth Railway. The date is April 13, 1962   [*B. J. Ashworth*

Below: 9711 crossing the Wye on its return trip to Ross after early morning shunting at Lydbrook in March 1965   [*B. J. Ashworth*

Above: The 4.45pm Taunton–Chard Central sidles out of Hatch, headed by
7436, on June 9, 1961   [*M. J. Fox*

Below: Chard Central. 9718, with two derelict looking coaches leaves the
weed-choked platform with the 4.07pm for Chard Junction in 1961   [*M. J. Fox*

Above: 3787 on an early morning Taunton–Chard train leaving Thornfalcon in
June 1962   [M. J. Fox

Below: 3787 climbs throatily out of Ilminster with a train bound for Chard in
March 1962   [M. J. Fox

Above: In marked contrast to the dereliction at Chard,
Ashburton looks a model of tidiness in this picture, taken
in August, 1945. The engine is 0–4–2 No. 4870

[*H. C. Casserley*

Below: The Moretonhampstead Branch, with its terminus
on the fringe of Dartmoor, was one of the most pleasant
and most under-photographed in the West. In this view,
4117 is seen near Lustleigh with the 2.15pm from Newton
Abbot   [*Peter F. Bowles*

Above: The typical branch terminus at Moretonhampstead.
[*Len's of Sutton*

Below: Meeting point—3705 at the Southern Region's Plymouth Friary, awaiting departure with a train for Yealmpton. On the right of the picture, taken in August 1945, is an LSWR M7 0–4–4T   [*H. C. Casserley*

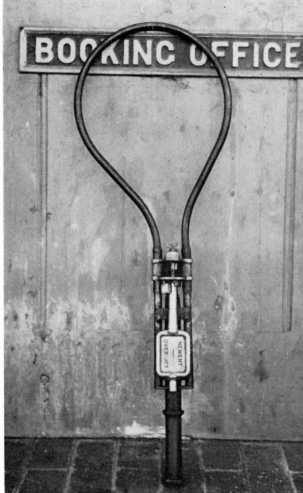

Above: Two items, both of which contributed to the Great
Western Branch Line scene   [*B. J. Ashworth*

Left: A delightfully rural picture of the Kington–Presteigne
goods in August 1964, a month before its demise
                                              [*B. J. Ashworth*

Above: Possibly the finest picture ever taken in the Forest of Dean. On a cold December morning in 1963, an 0–6–0T climbs the 1 in 30 between Coleford Junction and Coleford

[*B. J. Ashworth*

Right: The last NCB colliery in the Forest of Dean-Northern United, closed in December 1965. A 57xx propels some wagons into the sidings

[*B. J. Ashworth*

2286 waits in the bay at Ross-on-Wye in November 1963 before leaving for Lydbrook

[*B. J. Ashworth*

Above: Pontypridd Station. The 1.00pm Barry Island to Merthyr is about to take the right fork to Abercynon, whilst on the left, a 5600 0–6–2T heads for the Rhondda Valley   [S. Rickard

Below: Ex-Taff Vale 0–6–2T No. 379 nears Porthkerry on a Barry–Llantwit Major train on June 8, 1949   [J. C. Flemons

Above: Watford Crossing on February 16, 1957. Ex-Rhymney Railway 0–6–2T
No. 42 is about to traverse the Beddau Loop en route to Bargoed Pits
[S. Rickard

Below: The junction at Risca in May 1960, with 0–6–0T No. 6427 arriving with
a train from the Sirhowy Valley   [E. T. Gill

On the water's edge. 4575 class 2–6–2T No. 5524 passing Kingswear Crossing Halt with the 9.20am Kingswear–Exeter in May 1959 *[Peter F. Bowles*

Branch to Branch. 1470 leaving Churston, on the Kingswear
line, with the 11.13am auto-train for Brixham in March 1961
[*Peter F. Bowles*

Above: Just opposite Lelant lie Hayle Wharves, where 0–6–0T No. 9748 is seen in the early 1960s   [J. C. Beckett

Right: Climbing round the coast near Carbis Bay, 4570 tops the 1 in 60 with the St Erth–St Ives train in 1960
[M. Pope

Below: St Ives station, seen from Tregenna Hill. 2–6–2 No. 4547 is arriving from St Erth on September 29, 1956   [R. M. Casserley

A steam railcar on the Plymstock–Yealmpton branch, date
unknown   [Len's of Sutton

A photograph thought to have
been taken at Par in the 1880s.
The train is bound for Newquay
          [Collection of Morley Pascoe

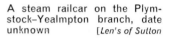

Another 2–4–0T, this time at
Avonwick, on the line from Brent
to Kingsbridge   [Len's of Sutton

Plymstock station around 1900,
with a train arriving from
Yealmpton. The Turnchapel
branch is on the right
                    [Len's of Sutton

A striking and effective picture of Barmouth Bridge. A
2–6–0 is heading south on an evening local to Dolgelly
in 1964   [*Malcolm Dunnett*

4575 2-6-2T No. 5550 hurries along near Cilgerran with a
Whitland to Cardigan train in 1963   [*M. J. Esau*

The up evening mail leaving Neyland for Johnston and
civilisation in the summer of 1963   [*M. J. Esau*

Above: A summer Saturday at Carmarthen in 1959. 2298 waits with the 2.40pm to Aberystwyth   [R. O. Tuck

Above, left: Meeting at the strangely named Strata Florida. An Aberystwyth–Carmarthen train is entering behind 2–6–0 No. 7312 on a summer Saturday in 1963   [M. J. Esau

Below, left: Aberayron, the terminus of the branch from Lampeter. (Originally the Lampeter, Aberayron and Newquay Light Railway). 7407 is about to leave to pick up milk tanks at Felin Fach on July 31, 1959   [R. O. Tuck

Left: A Dean goods and a high summer's day—there can have been few more pleasing sights. On June 24, 1952, No. 2351 turns north at Talyllyn Junction with the 5.05pm Brecon to Moat Lane   [*J. N. Westwood*

Right: Crossing point. 46516 at Builth Road (Low Level) with the 1.20pm Brecon–Moat Lane, while an 8F leaves the High Level on the 12.25 (SO) Shrewsbury–Swansea (Victoria)
     [*B. J. Ashworth*

Left: North of Three Cocks Junction, a 2MT No. 46507 heads south near Erwood on the 9.55am Moat Lane–Brecon in December 1962   [*A. Moyes*

Right: A trail of smoke portrays the path of a 5MT as it climbs towards Sugar Loaf Summit with the 7.45am Swansea–Shrewsbury on a grey, typically mid-Welsh morning in March 1961
     [*J. Spencer Gilks*

D

Right: This picture of 1466 between Morebath and Bampton sums up the beauty of this line on which so many people spent so many pleasant hours

[M. J. Fox

An Exe Valley local enters Tiverton from Exeter in August 1962
[M. J. Fox

Bampton station, with the 4.30pm arrival from Exeter about to leave as the 6.10pm to Exeter
[M. J. Fox

Right: 57xxs were used occasionally with the 14xx 0-4-2s—3659 is leaving Tiverton with the 9.25am to Exeter
[M. J. Fo.

Above: H. C. Casserley's well known picture of Hemyock, taken in 1929   [*H.C. Casserley*

Above, right: The Hemyock Branch epitomised the West Country scene—slow and peaceful. The train usually arrived, but it was no matter if it did not. 1466 leaves Tiverton Junction with its ex-Barry Railway coach (latterly an ex LNER brake) and a surprisingly good payload in August 1961   [*M. J. Fox*

Above, right: 1450, substituting for a failed diesel, heads for Hemyock to bring home the milk in December 1963   [*M. J. Fox*

Below, right: The 2.45pm Hemyock–Tiverton Junction beside the Culm at Culmstock in August 1962   [*M. J. Fox*

Another view of Hemyock station, this time in 1962   [*M. J. Fox*

Above: The railway on Portland—4624 at Easton with the 2.25pm freight to Portland and Weymouth on April 24, 1954   [J. W. Blanchard

Right, above: The last steam train from Bridport, an LCGB special, about to stall near Loders on January 21, 1967. The GWR's act of vengeance on that coaching stock . . .   [Ian Krause

Below: 1371 pulls the Channel Islands Boat Express through Weymouth in June 1950   [J. B. Snell

Right, below: A Victorian picture at Abbotsbury   [Len's of Sutton

The ultimate in rural branch line photography. Ben Ashworth's view of the Lydbrook goods at Kerne Bridge, from the top of an ash tree, has provided us with one of the most beautiful pictures taken in this country

[*B. J. Ashworth*

Above: The slopes of May Hill stand over the evening Gloucester–Hereford train as it climbs towards Lea Line Tunnel in June 1964
[B. J. Ashworth

Left: Another 2251 0–6–0, this time crossing the River Wye at Backney with the 16.30 Hereford–Gloucester, also in June 1964   [B. J. Ashworth

Above, right: Tinkering at Grange
Court Junction   [B. J. Ashworth

Right: November 20, 1963, with 2241
leaving Longhope for Hereford
                      [B. J. Ashworth

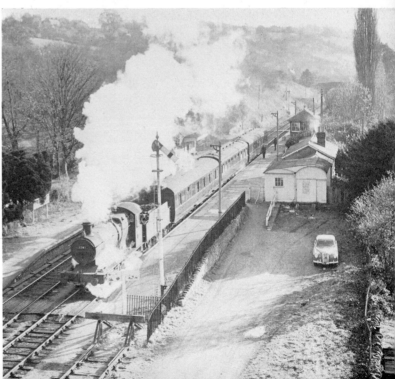

Above: A 72xx 2–8–2T trundles south from Abercwmboi towards Mountain Ash on September 23, 1964   [*B. J. Ashworth*

Right: Caerphilly Castle. A Cardiff–Senghenydd train is approaching Aber Junction Halt on February 16, 1957   [*S. Rickard*

Above: Under the landscaped tips at Dowlais Cae Harris, 0–6–2T No. 5662 approaches with the 3.15pm from Nelson and Llancaiach   [*Gerald T. Robinson*

Right, top: The railhead at Senghenydd—one of the surprisingly few railway pictures one sees incorporating South Wales's once great industry   [*Richard Doran*

Right, bottom: A train of coal empties on the Roath Branch of the former Taff Vale Railway, situated on the northern outskirts of Cardiff, in April 1955   [*S. Rickard*

Above: A freight from Brecon to Merthyr crossing Pont-sarn Viaduct in March 1961
[J. Spencer Gilks

Below: Pentir–Rhiw, halfway stage of the seven mile climb to Torpantau. 9676 is approaching on a short freight
[B. J. Ashworth

Above: 4679, on the 12.10pm Brecon–Newport, approaches the summit of the 1 in 38 from Talybont at Torpantau Tunnel on November 2, 1962 *[B. J. Ashworth*

Right: The clouds hang low over Torpantau, as the driver of 9679 exchanges tokens en route for Merthyr *[B. J. Ashworth*

E

Above: 1445 propelling the 5.40pm Tenbury Wells–Craven Arms west of Tenbury on August 1, 1959   [M. Mensing

Left: 2516 approaches Cleobury Mortimer on a West Midlands Railtour on May 21, 1955   [Donald Kelk

Right: 4613 approaches Bromyard in June 1964 with the 5.40 pm for Worcester   [John R. P. Hunt

Left, below: Ten years after. Admiralty and BR trains at Cleobury Mortimer in March 1965   [Andrew Muckley

Below: GW Railcar No. 19 near Tenbury with the 6.22pm Kidderminster–Woofferton   [M. Mensing

Railcars took over the Marlow–Bourne End branch in July 1962. 1421 was photographed at Marlow shortly before this   [*Brian Haresnape*

Not a branch at all, but a rare picture of a Westbourne Park–Northolt train at Old Oak Lane Halt in June 1947   [*H. C. Casserley*

Ex-GW Railcars, Nos. 33 and 38 at Cowley, on the Uxbridge branch on
September 24, 1960
[M. Pope

Another 0–4–0 No. 219 leaving Brentham on a
local train in 1930   [J. E. Kite

0–4–2T No. 1486 near Colnbrook, with a Staines–
West Drayton train in 1929   [J. E. Kite

A Kidlington to Woodstock train on Thrupp curve in February 1954   *[D. D. Beattie*

Great Western at Abingdon in May 1952. The engine, 1437, would appear to be least elderly of the assembly

[J. B. Snell

The Woodstock Branch bay at Kidlington in 1952

[J. B. Snell

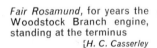

Fair Rosamund, for years the Woodstock Branch engine, standing at the terminus

{H. C. Casserley

Above: On a fine evening in July 1953, 4558 hurries the 6.10pm Fairford–Oxford train past Wolvercote Junction   [E. D. Bruton

Right: Fairford Terminus in 1962, with 2221 waiting to leave for Oxford   [D. Holmes

Above: Evening near Cholsey. 1447 heads a train from
Wallingford in August 1958   [*J. A. Coiley*

Top: Didcot, Newbury and Southampton. 4–4–0 No. 3266 *Amyas* arrives at Winchester (Chesil) on a train from Didcot. Centre: 0–6–0 No. 2573 waits at Lambourn on September 5, 1952. Bottom: 2055 simmers at Watlington after arrival from Princes Risborough shortly before the outbreak of war in 1939   [*H. C. Casserley*

Two views on the Burry Port and Gwendraeth Valley line. In the first, 1957 and 1967 sit at Cwm Mawr, whilst the lower picture shows 1967 awaiting departure at Burry Port. Both were taken on July 7, 1947   [*H. C. Casserley*

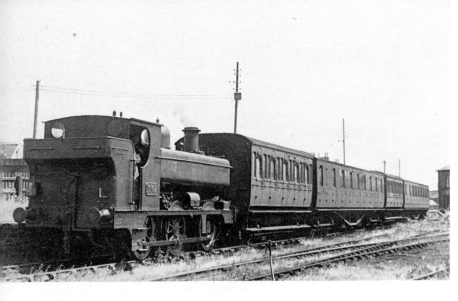

Blaengarw in 1952. 3668 has just arrived on a train from Tondu
[*H. C. Casserley*

5570 class 0–6–0PT No. 9666 nears Cymmer Afan with the 7.00am R & SB
Junction–Abergwynfi class 9 in August 1964   [Gerald T. Robinson

A general view of Tondu North Junction in July 1952   [S. Rickard

Left: Hengoed Viaduct, with 4108 crossing at the head of the 10.55am
Pontypool Road–Neath in July 1963   [*John White*

0–6–2T No. 6605 nears Quakers Yard (High Level) on the
4.20pm Neath–Hengoed on August 20, 1952

Left: The most unhealthy looking structures at Quaker's Yard. A Pannier tank is seen on the 11.19am Neath–Pontypool Road in March 1958
[*S. Rickard*

Right: Two 2–8–0Ts Nos. 5222 and 5239 assault Glyn Neath bank with a westbound coal train on July 21, 1961   [*S. A. Leleux*

The view from the viaduct. A 5600 0–6–2T is descending from Penrhos Junction, and above this the line from Penrhos Junction to Cadoxton which crosses the viaduct. The Cardiff–Pontypridd Line is in the foreground

[S. Rickard

Winter's day at Taffs Well. A train of empties from Cadoxton to Penallta Colliery is crossing Walnut Tree Viaduct

[*S. Rickard*

1420 at Titley Junction after a trip up the Presteigne branch
in August 1964   [B. J. Ashworth

Bullock's Mill Crossing a month later. 1420 is returning to
Hereford from Kington   [B. J. Ashworth

eft: Tea break at Kington
                    [Andrew Muckley

Left: The crew of 6437 share a joke between trains at Berkeley Road   [B. J. Ashworth

Right: 6437 again—this time leaving Berkeley with the 4.55pm Berkeley Road to Sharpness. The date is May 17, 1963
[B. J. Ashworth

Right: The remains of the Severn Bridge, before it was dismantled in 1967. Severn Bridge station is in the fore-ground   [B. J. Ashworth

Scrap metal for Sharpness leaving Berkeley Road behind a 14xx in July 1964 [B. J. Ashworth

Above: Freight from Gloucester Docks to Dymock between Barber's Bridge and Molswick on a chilly December day in 1963   [B. J. Ashworth

Below: Monmouth (Troy), looking east. The line to Ross curves away to the left, while the Chepstow and Forest of Dean lines are on the right   [M. G. D. Farr

Above: 9619 at Tintern Quarry on the Chepstow–Monmouth line on September 22, 1964   [*M. R. C. Price*

Below: The magnificent scenery of the Wye Valley is shown to good effect in this picture of 6412 leaving St Briavels for Monmouth on June 2, 1962
[*J. Spencer Gilks*

Three views of the Minera Branch from Wrexham. 9610, banked by 9630 is seen climbing to Minera, and the pair were photographed near Brymbo with the return loaded wagons on May 7, 1966

[*David E. Gouldthorp*

Above: Shunting at Blaenau Ffes-
tiniog in March 1954   [*J. B. Snell*

Left: 5810 waiting with a train from
Bala Junction in 1953
        [*H. C. Casserley*

Below: 7442 rattles along near
Glyndyfrdwy on a Ruabon–Bala
train in June 1956   [*J. B. Snell*

Right: Crossing at Drws-y-Nant
        [*Malcolm Dunnett*

Manor on the Cambrian—a Saturday extra climbs through Cemmaes Road
in August 1963

[*Malcolm Dunnett*

Crossing the Dovey at Dovey Junction   [*Malcolm Dunnett*

Above: An ex-Cambrian Railway 0-6-0 working back to Pwllheli from Portmadoc in August 1954   [J. B. Snell

Right: The last up "Cambrian Coast Express" throws up a vast column of smoke as it climbs the 1 in 52 to Talerddig behind 75033 on March 4, 1967   [R. I. Vallance

Below: A southbound train climbing to Friog Avalanche Shelter in 1964   [Malcolm Dunnett

The beauty of Devon. 4591 climbs the 1 in 55 from Liddaton Halt to Lydford
with the 10.15am Launceston–Plymouth on June 9, 1962   [*Peter F. Bowles*

Above and below: Fifty year contrast at Looe—Pun intended! [*Len's of Sutton*]

Above: Moorswater Yard, from the viaduct. Beyond the shed the line formerly continued to Cheesewring Quarries and Caradon [*J. B. Snell*

Left: Looe station on July 10, 1924; the engine is 0-6-0 No. 1941 [*H. C. Casserley*

Above: The 10.45 from Looe climbs from Coombe Junction to Liskeard on July 9, 1960. The main line from Plymouth crosses the viaduct behind
[J. Spencer Gilks

Work and heat at Abercynon   [*B. J. Ashworth*

100

Heat, but little work, at Treharris   *[B. J. Ashworth*

The 10.50am Cheltenham (St James)–Kingham
climbing the Chelt Valley near Dowdeswell
behind 5173 on March 19, 1962   [B. J. Ashworth

Right, top: Two years later—demolishing the
line at Notgrove, after the contractor's loco had
failed   [B. J. Ashworth

Right, bottom: On July 7, 1961, the Andoversford
–Swindon pick-up threads Chedworth Wood on
the Mand SWJ with 9740 at the head
                                    [B. J. Ashworth

GWR No. 540 at Blagdon in 1929 with a train for Congresbury

[*H. C. Casserley*

Tetbury in April 1955, terminus of the branch from Kemble

[*H. C. Casserley*

1400 entering Calne from Chippenham

[*Len's of Sutton*

Above: The 4.20pm Ledbury Junction–Worcester propels
itself away on April 18, 1953   [N. E. Mitchell

Left: Old Ynysybwl, on the
branch from Clydach and
Pontypridd, in September
1951   [H. C. Casserley

Above: Falmouth station, with 5500 arriving on the 10.50am ex-Newquay and 12.03pm ex Truro on May 17, 1959   [M. Mensing

Left: County 4–6–0 No. 1006 struggles up the 1 in 37 from Par to Luxulyan with through coaches from Paddington to Newquay in June 1960   [J. Spencer Gilks

Below: Fowey, terminus of the branch from Lostwithiel, in May 1935
                                                                                                [H. C. Casserley

Perranwell signal box, on the Truro–Falmouth branch   [*Len's of Sutton*

Abbotsbury in the 19th century   [*Len's of Sutton*

Malmesbury terminus   [*Len's of Sutton*

One of the rare pictures taken on the Hooton to West Kirby branch. 1457 arrives at West Kirby (Birkenhead Joint) station on April 20, 1954

[R. M. Casserley

Another rarity—the Clee Hill Mineral Railway (former GWR–LMS Joint). 4678 struggles up to Bitterley with the thrice weekly train to Ludlow in August 1956
[*G. F. Bannister*

"And, as the sun sinks slowly in the West . . . ! !", so a local approaches
Portmadoc in 1964. And finally . .. *[Malcolm Dunnett*

Western Region

British Railways Board

Transport Act 1962

Withdrawal of
railway passenger services

**The services will be withdrawn
on and from Monday, 2nd November, 1964**

The Minister of Transport has given his
consent to the Board's proposal to
discontinue all passenger train services
between **GLOUCESTER (Central)** and
HEREFORD and from the following
stations and halts:-

OAKLE STREET	WESTON-UNDER-PENYARD HALT
GRANGE COURT	ROSS-ON-WYE
BLAISDON HALT	FAWLEY
LONGHOPE	BALLINGHAM
MITCHELDEAN ROAD	HOLME LACY

The terms of the Minister's consent can
be inspected at local booking offices

The date the services will be withdrawn
will be announced later.

. . . Epitaph   [*B. J. Ashworth*